Original title:
Beyond the Front Door

Copyright © 2025 Creative Arts Management OÜ
All rights reserved.

Author: Gabriel Kingsley
ISBN HARDBACK: 978-1-80587-107-1
ISBN PAPERBACK: 978-1-80587-577-2

The Dichotomy of Comfort

Inside my cozy pants I dwell,
Soft as a marshmallow shell.
The world outside can be a fright,
But oh, that couch feels oh so right!

The mailman waves, he's dressed in grey,
I wave back without dismay.
To step outside would end this bliss,
But pizza's calling, can't resist!

My feline friend patrols the space,
Guarding the realm with a scowling face.
He knows the danger lurking near:
The vacuum cleaner is full of fear!

So here I sit, a rebel true,
Wrapped in my blanket, thoughts askew.
The air seems fresh, but oh, the chore—
Who needs adventure? Not anymore!

Reflections on the Other Side

A doormat tells a tale,
Of shoes that tripped and fell.
The cat thinks it's a stage,
For her illustrious spell.

The mailbox smiles shyly,
At letters lined in a row.
Each one holds a mystery,
Of who sent it and why so?

A Boundless Invitation

The garden gnome waves wildly,
As squirrels plan their heist.
A party in the tulips,
Intrigue at every tryst.

A neighbor peeks through blinds,
With cookies stacked on high.
"Come on over, bring a chair!"
Said with a wink and a sigh.

Imagined Journeys Await

The porch swing creaks with laughter,
Imagining it's a plane.
To France for cheese and laughter,
Or a beach to dance in rain.

Birds chatter in a conference,
Discussing seeds and snacks.
While I sip on my lemonade,
They plot their daring flacks.

Unfolding the Unexpected

The garden hose is tangled,
Like thoughts from last night's dream.
It squirts me with a giggle,
Oh, this is quite the scheme!

A package on the doorstep,
Is it treasure or a prank?
An octopus in a box,
Now who would drive that tank?

Walkways to Infinity

There's a garden gnome, standing tall,
Chasing squirrels, he's bound to fall.
With a wink and a nod, he plots his spree,
Wondering how much fun it could be.

The lawnmower sings, hits a high note,
While Mrs. Smith tries to float a boat.
With a splash and a giggle, she splutters away,
Only to find the cat wants to play.

The Lure of Untrodden Paths

There's a puddle calling, come take a leap,
But watch out for the mud, it's far too deep.
Old Mr. Thompson just took a dive,
Now his laugh echoes, he feels alive!

The trees are whispering soft little lies,
Telling tales of adventures, under bright skies.
While squirrels plan parties just out of sight,
I swear I saw one, dressed up in white!

Frame of Hidden Stories

Behind the bushes, a dog plays peek,
With the neighbor's cat, it's quite the sneak.
Caught with a paw on the fence's top,
Both tumble down—oh, flop! flop! flop!

The fence holds secrets of a time gone by,
When kids on bikes could soar and fly.
And painted rocks tell tales of woe,
Of gnomes lost in battles, to the lawn they go!

The Light Just Outside

At twilight's dance, the fireflies glow,
A disco for bugs, with quite a show.
When Gramps comes out in his bright pink robe,
Twisting and turning, he steals the globe!

The grill's on fire with a hot dog flair,
But Auntie June's hair—oh, the smoke in the air!
With laughter and chatter, our spirits soar,
It's a party of giggles, who could want more?

Faded Welcome Mats

The mat outside is brown and worn,
Where all the muddrops have been born.
It yells, 'Welcome!' with a faded cheer,
Yet one more guest, I truly fear.

The doorbell laughs, it knows the game,
As friends bring chaos, no one's the same.
The dog's in charge, he steals the show,
While family frisbees fly like a crow.

Where Shadows Linger

Shadows dance in the afternoon sun,
Riddles and giggles, oh what fun!
The chairs invite ghosts of meals long gone,
As I chase the cat, she's already drawn.

Creaks and squeaks, quite the lively crew,
Whispered secrets known by just a few.
The kitchen spills laughter, like flour in the air,
While echoes of mishaps play without a care.

The Silence After Goodbye

A heavy door that swings shut tight,
Leaves behind echoes of silly delight.
Who knew a hug could cause such a mess?
Now crumpled pizza boxes clutter, no less.

I eye the couch, a fortress of crumbs,
While the clock chuckles; time gently hums.
Yet in this quiet, my heart does a flip,
Imagining next week's pizza trip.

Landscapes of the Unseen

In corners where dust bunnies come alive,
Adventures await, they secretively thrive.
Under the couch, a kingdom is made,
Where socks have gone, and laughter won't fade.

The fridge guards treasures, half-eaten cake,
While notes on the wall share a fun, funny take.
Hide-and-seek echoed in the rear,
Life's sweetest trick, where we play without fear.

Echoes of the Outside

The neighbors yell, the lawnmower roars,
Someone's dog just knocked down the doors.
Children squeal as they race in the sun,
I sip my tea, they're having such fun.

A cat in a hat walks down the street,
Chasing a mouse on tiny, quick feet.
Laughter echoes, life's silly display,
Through the window, I watch this grand ballet.

A Journey Past the Frame

I gear up for adventure, what will it bring?
Greeted by the mailman, wearing his bling.
He hands me a package, filled with delight,
 Bubble wrap pops! What a silly sight!

I spot a squirrel, wearing a cape,
 Dashing for nuts, oh what a escape!
What lies on the curb? An odd yellow shoe,
 Worn by who? Maybe it's just a clue!

The Veil of Evening Light

As twilight descends, the crickets all sing,
A door opens wide—what fun it can bring!
Fireflies dance with their flickering glow,
 Whispers of mischief begin to flow.

A raccoon in goggles raiding the trash,
Dances in shadows, oh what a dash!
The grill's still warm, we roast marshmallows,
 Under the stars, we enjoy our jellows!

Footprints on the Threshold

Footprints of summer, mud on my mat,
Children still giggling, dogs playing with that!
Dust bunnies gather, the threshold a mess,
Yet laughter fills moments, nothing but blessed.

The doorbell rings—it's a surprise party!
Balloons fly in, it's getting quite hearty.
What joy behind me, what fun lies ahead,
Life is a riddle, and merrily spread!

Within the Citadel of Silence

In the fortress of my home, I dwell,
Where laundry piles up, it's quite a smell.
The vacuum's a monster hiding in the hall,
Waiting for my bravest call.

The cat claims the throne, a fuzzy little king,
With fur all around, it's a real fuzzy thing.
The dishes stack high like a tower of doom,
While I scheme of escape to the bright, sunny room.

The Threshold of Transformation

I step from my haven, it's flip-flop season,
The mailbox is lurking, a postman's reason.
An Amazon package? Oh what a delight!
Another odd gadget—will it make my day bright?

I dance through the garden with weeds and a smile,
While neighbors peer over, wondering what's my style.
I sing at the top of my lungs to the breeze,
To the squirrels and the robins who seem less at ease.

Whispers of the Unexpected

A knock on the door, who could it be?
A delivery man with a package for me!
I open it wide, and what do I see?
A life-size cardboard cutout from a movie spree!

The doorbell rings thrice, it's the pizza guy's cheer,
I answer in pajamas, with crumbs from last year.
He looks at me funny, I'm trying to explain,
That the dog is a barker, he's simply insane!

Yearning for Escape

I dream of a journey to a beach far and wide,
Where sunburns don't happen, and troubles subside.
But the best I can manage is a stroll to the park,
With a frisbee and sandwich, and a wild, barking lark.

Yet here I am stuck with my rollers and mop,
While fantasies of travel make my heart stop.
I'll laugh at this chaos, my humorous fate,
As I conquer the laundry pile—oh it's getting late!

Footsteps on Forgotten Steps

A knock that echoes softly through,
A shoe left dangling, oh, it's true.
With every creak and squeak we hear,
A ghostly dance, or just my beer?

Unexpected guests, a pizza guy,
Wearing clown shoes, oh my, oh my!
He trips and falls, we laugh aloud,
In our small realm, he's quite the crowd.

An old dog snores, he thinks he's brave,
Patting his back, we all misbehave.
With socks upon our hands, we play,
A sock war waged, let's save the day!

When afternoon turns into night,
The shadows tease, a silly fright.
A place where laughter seems to soar,
What fun awaits behind that door!

A Portal to Possibility

When you twist the knob, what do you see?
A mountain of laundry, just for me.
Socks in pairs? Oh no, what's that!
A portal opens, it's a cat!

It pounces forth like it's a game,
Chasing dust bunnies, wild and tame.
With every leap and every bound,
Who knew such joy on the ground?

A broom left standing, can it fly?
I swear, I saw it wave goodbye!
Whirling around, it took a chance,
Invited all for a long dance.

Adventures brewing in the air,
We thought we'd find some treasure there.
Instead, just crumbs, a couple of mice,
Still, what a portal—oh, so nice!

Inside the Quietude

In the stillness, chaos reigns,
With sprinkles of laughter, all the gains.
A chair that squeaks, a dog that snores,
The perfect mix behind these doors.

Silence broken by a sneeze,
'Twas just a dust cloud—below your knees!
Best take cover; it's bound to rain,
Popcorn flew, but it's all in the game.

A tickle fight breaks out for fun,
Now everyone's a sprightly one.
Who knew that quiet could be loud?
With giggles bright, we are so proud.

Between the hush and sudden shout,
You'll never guess what lurks about.
In this nook where we reside,
Laughter and whispers, side by side!

The Edge of Discovery

A crack below the latch reveals,
A kingdom ripe with banana peels.
Explorers gather, backpacks tight,
Is that a mouse? Oh, what a sight!

In corners old, and cobwebs wan,
We find a treasure—an old prawn,
It's smell defies the rules of fate,
But still, it's cause to celebrate!

A door that creaks, a stair that squeaks,
Unearthing quirks—oh, so unique!
A family photo, all askew,
What's that? A finger? Eek! A shoe?

From trinkets small to odd-shaped rocks,
Each little find unlocks the stocks.
Adventure calls, and off we dash,
At the edge of wonder, and a wink, a flash!

A Door Left Ajar

A door swings wide, a cheeky grin,
Who knows what mayhem lurks within?
Is it a cat or an old lost shoe?
Secretly plotting, watch what they do.

The wind whispers tales of what could be,
An impromptu party for you and me.
With snacks in hand and a clumsy dance,
No one can resist this wild romance.

A sock on the floor, a hat on the ledge,
All things are possible, let's make a pledge.
To leap through the chaos, to spin and twirl,
In a world where laughter can always unfurl.

So, peek through that crack, take a good look,
In this door's wild world, not a minute's mistook.
Adventure awaits in the joy and the mess,
Where even a sneeze becomes pure happiness!

Hushed Conversations at Dusk

Chatting in whispers, what secrets we share,
Under the glow of the soft evening air.
A raccoon's debate, a squirrel's grand plan,
All the wild critters have gotta take a stand.

A butterfly lands on a nearby leaf,
To join in the chatter, we're all in disbelief.
The world's on the edge, listening in tight,
As the crickets all join for a late-night plight.

They giggle and gossip, plot mischief anew,
While I sit and marvel, thinking, 'Who knew?'
In the shadows of dusk, where giggles abound,
Life is a circus, and laughter's the sound.

Each twilight brings murmurs, tangled and sweet,
A treasure of tales rolling soft at our feet.
So raise a soft toast to the whimsy we find,
In the hush of the night, where all minds unwind.

The Dance of Arrival

In comes the guest, a wild twirl of flair,
With mismatched socks and a wild-eyed stare.
They trip on the mat, with a laugh and a yelp,
Announcing their joy like a sprightly kelp.

Beneath the bright lights, they shimmy and sway,
Turning the room into a cabaret.
A dog joins the fun, trying to leap,
In a whirlwind of joy, it's hard not to weep.

With snacks flying high, and voices a crowd,
All worries dissolve, laughter's unbowed.
As the clock ticks away, we dance and we spin,
In a house full of friends, let the madness begin.

When it's time to leave, we hold on tight,
To the dance of arrival, the savagely bright.
So here's to the moments that make us alive,
Let chaotic arrivals be how we thrive!

The Stillness of Inquiry

Peeking around corners, what will I find?
A toaster with secrets, or a curious mind?
Who left those shoes there, stacked so absurd?
The sock's lost its partner, it's quite a big bird.

With a notepad in hand, I take notes in haste,
Every odd trinket has its own spicy taste.
Mysteries linger in the midst of the fun,
Each item a story, a race just begun.

What does this button do? I must investigate,
Is it a portal, or just food on a plate?
And those empty pizza boxes stacked high?
They whisper of laughter and late-night pie.

In the stillness, I ponder with glee and delight,
This house full of questions is sparkling bright.
So here's to the wonders that lay all around,
In the corners of curious homes, joy is found.

Chasing Light Beyond the Frame

In a house where shadows play,
I trip on shoes in disarray.
The dog is snoring, quite a show,
As daylight sneaks in, oh so slow.

Dust bunnies dance in sunlit beams,
Are they alive, or just my dreams?
The cat now rules the coffee mug,
With a swagger and a little shrug.

Mom's old hat now on my head,
Looks like I've joined the grumpy shed.
The fridge hums tunes, a sweet delight,
While I explore this morning light.

In every corner, laughter reigns,
With cereal spills and little stains.
A world of wonder I can see,
Right here, it seems, is where I'll be.

Echoes of Yesterday

There's a ghost in my cereal bowl,
Sipping milk, not feeling whole.
Last week's pizza on the floor,
Dreams of diets forever more.

The cat gives a look, oh so sly,
As I fumble, trying to fly.
Old socks whisper tales of their day,
Cursed in the wash, they're here to stay.

Mom's old camera takes a snap,
Who knew it had a hidden trap?
Images of me with hair like hay,
Forever etched in disarray.

The time machine's stuck in the hall,
Where I trip and tumble, take a fall.
Each echo brings a laugh or shriek,
Adventures await, no need to sneak.

What Lies in Wait

Behind the curtain, something stirs,
A lone sock laughs as the humor blurs.
The plants are plotting garden schemes,
While I tiptoe through dusty dreams.

A coffee pot sings like a diva,
As I see the latest kitchen fever.
Spilled juice looks like modern art,
Or just a lesson, my daily part.

Cookies hide in crinkled wraps,
While I navigate around the traps.
The ghosts of snacks past laugh with glee,
In this world where all's so free.

Each closet holds forgotten lore,
With board games and trinkets galore.
What lies in wait, I do not know,
But I'll trip in sunshine, enjoying the show.

The Unfolding Horizon

The mailbox greets me with a grin,
Full of coupons that could never win.
The garden gnomes plan a parade,
With each tiny detail carefully laid.

Socks on the porch wave hello,
As butterflies dance, quite a show.
Neighbors shout jokes over the fence,
With laughter mixing in every tense.

The barbecue grill plots a feast,
While ants declare, 'We're called at least!'
A squirrel debates a nutty plan,
An acorn looks to become a fan.

In this unfolding scene, so bright,
I laugh with joy, in sheer delight.
Life rolls its eyes and says, 'Oh, come!'
And here, every moment feels like fun.

Threshold Whispers

There's a world outside my home,
Where lawn gnomes plot and roam.
They speak in whispers, oh so sly,
About the neighbors' cat named Pie.

I peek outside, what do I see?
A squirrel dancing like it's free.
He twirls and leaps with wild delight,
I laugh, it's quite the funny sight!

The mailman trips, he fumbles fast,
He's dodging kittens, oh what a blast!
He yells, "Not again!" with comical flair,
As packages fly through the air.

And on the curb, a dog wears shades,
With a coolness that never fades.
He winks at me as if to say,
"Adventure's out there, let's not delay!"

The World Awaits Beyond

I opened my door to a chorus of birds,
Who sang of plans far more absurd.
They wore tiny hats, what a view!
Gathered to discuss the day's debut.

A squirrel in a top hat gave a toast,
"Here's to nuts, our favorite boast!"
The bunnies cheered, with a thump and hop,
In this whimsical world, you just can't stop.

Behind the fence, I saw a scene,
A lawn chair race, oh so keen!
With garden gnomes as field marshals proud,
The laughter erupted, oh my, so loud!

I joined the fun with my flip-flop shoes,
Racing with spirits, how could I lose?
In this land of silly delight,
Every moment feels just right!

Unseen Horizons

A garden waits, where giggles bloom,
With daisies planning to break through gloom.
They whisper tales of sun and cheer,
As butterflies dance, oh so near.

A hedgehog in glasses reads the news,
"More rain today, wear your shoes!"
He rolls his eyes, so well-informed,
While ants plan parades, perfectly formed.

The grass seems ticklish, giggling bright,
As the sun dips low, preparing for night.
I trip on a leaf, what a clumsy plight,
But laughter erupts, it feels just right!

With neighbors peeking over their fences,
Catching the joy of nature's pretenses.
We join together, a whimsical crew,
Helloo! to the universe, a world anew!

Steps into the Unknown

Each step I take, what will I find?
A treasure of chuckles, oh so kind.
A cat in pajamas, yawning awake,
Decides to follow my curious stake.

The sidewalk springs with lively tales,
Of prancing dogs and fluttering sails.
A kid in a cape flies by with speed,
Chasing after laughter, true superhero creed.

There's a turtle racing on a skateboard,
With dreams of fame, not to be ignored.
While pigeons gather for a game of chess,
With rooks made of bread, oh what a mess!

So off I wander, hat upon head,
Discovering stories where laughter's led.
In this realm of folly, I'm never alone,
For every adventure is joyfully sown.

Moments in the In-Between

I stand and peer through window gaps,
Awaiting life, there's fun in traps.
The cat jumps high to chase a bird,
While I fantasize churning curds.

Delivery guy, he looks confused,
My pants are strange, my hair abused.
He wonders if this is my style,
I grin and say, 'Just for a while!'

My neighbor wrestles with his gate,
It squeaks and groans—it seals his fate.
He yells at it with wobbly hands,
As I chuckle, making new plans.

The world outside, it spins and dances,
While I practice all my glances.
The jester here, in my abode,
Finds fun in every little code.

The Longing Beyond the Latch

My dog is barking at the leaves,
Pretending he's a knight, he believes.
He guards the castle—my dear yard,
While squirrels plot beneath the guard.

A cake just baked, but oh, what's that?
A fly has claimed it—what a brat!
I swat and swirl, all in good jest,
Now it's a game; this is the best!

The mailman waves with quiet glee,
Unaware of my tightrope spree.
I dance on tiptoes, acting grand,
As packages drift in my hand.

Through wooden frames, the laughter peeks,
With every knock, the fun just sneaks.
What secrets hide behind that latch,
As I giggle at each new catch.

Wholesome Discontent

I sip my tea, it's far too hot,
My shirt is sticky—what a plot!
The toaster's jammed, it laughs at me,
As crumbs scatter like confetti.

The fridge hums loud; it's having fun,
As leftover soup calls, 'Hey, come run!'
I pause but just for one more bite,
It's a low-carb diet, so polite.

The garden weeds have claimed their reign,
I wrestle with them, all in vain.
My neighbor shouts, "Come see my blooms!"
I grin and wave from my facepalm rooms.

In this delightfully messy sport,
I stand alone, no last resort.
The sun comes in, and laughter springs,
In each discontent, the joy it brings.

A Whirlwind of New Horizons

An umbrella opens in a gust,
It flips and spins; oh, what a thrust!
I twirl about like some grand fool,
As raindrops play their watery pool.

My umbrella's lost its well-made grip,
It dances off—I lose my trip!
A stampede of shoes on the street,
As I tear along, a comic feat.

Neighbors peep from behind their glass,
Amused by how the raindrops sass.
Their plants grow strong, while I will sway,
In puddles deep, I choose to play.

A whirlwind brings more than just rain,
It gives us laughter, skips mundane.
In chaos loud, so bright and free,
New horizons bloom—just wait and see!

The Interstice of Shadows

In the hallway, I find my shoes,
They seem to mock me, what to choose?
Left or right? My head shall spin,
It's just a path, where do I begin?

The cat stares from upon the stair,
Teasingly flicks its tail in air.
I trip on socks, a dangerous game,
And wonder if they're all to blame.

Out the window, the world looks bright,
But oh, the yard's a feral sight!
With weeds that dance and grass that twirls,
I'd rather deal with catnip curls!

There's laughter echoing through the hall,
As I balance, nearly take a fall.
But in this chaos, joy I find,
In every step, the absurdity's kind.

A Step Into the Ether

A door is cracked, a breeze comes in,
With every creak, my nerves begin.
What lies behind that wooden wall?
Could it be nothing, or a cat's call?

After all, the carpet's worn,
From battles fought, and snacks forsworn.
I tiptoe forth, all senses keen,
What mysteries await, unforeseen?

A dust bunny rolls like a rogue knight,
In quest for crumbs, a noble fight.
I watch and laugh at this grand spree,
Is home just a stage for quirk and glee?

The shadows twist, they start to dance,
Inviting me into their little prance.
I join the fun, then realize too late,
I've stepped on a toy, destined for fate!

Adventures in the Mundane

The dishes piled like a mountain high,
A quest for spoons—oh me, oh my!
In every corner, dishes wait,
For rescue from this endless fate.

An errant sock seems to conspire,
To jump aboard my laundry fire!
It wriggles free, a slippery foe,
And scampers off, think I don't know?

Out the back, the garden's fair,
But weeds play games without a care.
I chase them down, they giggle anew,
Victory's sweet, but not quite true.

With every chore, a circus grows,
In puddles splash where no one goes.
Each mundane task, a chance to play,
In the great escapade of every day.

The Gateway of Dreams

A portal opens, I take a peek,
Inside my house, what joys are sleek?
I find adventure in the bin,
Where lost old toys start to spin!

The couch transforms into a ship,
Where cushions crew take a daring trip.
My cat the captain with a glare,
As I sail on imaginary air.

The kitchen's a lab, oh what fun,
With pots and pans ready to run!
I stir a potion, a laugh out loud,
As cookies bloom, from chaos endowed!

A knock at the door, adventure calls,
I'll leave these dreams for the outside brawls.
But every trip's a funny sketch,
In my world where whimsy's a fetch!

The Call of Unexplored Realms

A door creaks open wide,
Dust and socks collide.
An old cat leaps out,
With a look of doubt.

What lies in the unknown?
A garden overgrown?
A gopher with a hat?
I swear I saw a rat!

Mysteries await me there,
With adventures to share.
But mops might be a trap,
And that's a sneaky map!

So I stand and stare down,
At the mess that's my town.
Tomorrow I'll explore,
But for now? I'll just snore!

Crossing the Visible Line

The sidewalk's just a line,
Step over? Never mine!
That hedgehog looks quite wise,
With a sparkle in his eyes.

But what's this, a gate?
Is trouble my fate?
The neighbors shout in fright,
"Why are you out at night?"

With a waddle and a hop,
A gopher starts to bop.
He waves with tiny hands,
And goofy, silly plans.

So I tiptoe and slide,
Down the path, I decide.
If chaos be the plan,
Sign me up, here I am!

Shadows Beneath the Sill

Shadows dance and sway,
Where dust bunnies play.
A broom flies by in fright,
It's a wild, wacky night!

Underneath the sill,
Something gives me a chill.
Could it be a mouse?
Or my neighbor's old spouse?

With a wig and a grin,
She just wants to win!
Hopscotch on the floor,
She cackles, "Want more?"

In this house of odd,
Craziness is the cod.
Step softly in the hall,
For you might trip and fall!

The Limit of Familiarity

My garden's just a yard,
But today it feels hard.
The hedges grew a limb,
And I fell in a whim.

What's this strange terrain?
With carrots writing rain?
Astronauts in the grass,
Flinging pies en masse!

I'd tread light as air,
But there's cream everywhere.
Loud are the radish cheers,
As I face my great fears.

In the end, what a sight!
Picking skin off in fright.
Perhaps I'll stick around,
For laughs that can be found!

Inviting the Unknown

A knock on the door, who could it be?
A cat with a hat, or maybe a flea?
I peek through the window, my heart in a spin,
Could it be my neighbor, or a mischievous twin?

The door swings open, what a surprise!
A goat in a tutu, oh how it flies!
It waltzes right in, like it's part of the crew,
I laugh as it dances, what else can I do?

A sign on the wall says 'Welcome and Stay!'
With snacks for the goat, all debts washed away.
The world is a stage, and my house, a grand play,
With animals frolicking, brightening the day.

So here's to the wild, the silly and strange,
To moments like this, I wouldn't exchange.
For life's little wonders, make us feel light,
Especially the ones that show up at night!

The Weight of a Doorknob

My doorknob is heavy, it feels like a lead,
It stares at me sternly, as if it has said:
"Open me gently, or I might just explode!"
I rustle my keys, it laughs, a fine road!

As I turn it with care, a creak like a squeal,
Could it be haunted? It's tough to conceal.
But out into the world, I bravely must peer,
Ready for chaos or a puppy, oh dear!

Once outside, it chuckles, I swear that it grins,
At all of my foes, my fears, and my sins.
But with a swift yank and a pulling with might,
I've opened the door, much to my delight.

A parade of ducklings now waddle and quake,
My doorknob just giggles, for goodness' sake!
"There's always a weight," it said with a sigh,
"But laughter returns when you're willing to try!"

Steps into the Unfamiliar

Each step from my door, a question, a dare,
Will I find a treasure? Or something quite rare?
My shoes squeak like mice, as I tiptoe outside,
To discover the wonders the world tries to hide.

The sidewalk's a puzzle, the trees have a hunch,
Will I meet a giraffe, or a squirrel with a lunch?
I laugh at my thoughts, it's all just a game,
What fun is adventure if I'm always the same?

The bushes are rustling, is something awake?
A hedgehog in sunglasses, for goodness' sake!
It struts like it's fancy, it sneezes, oh dear,
Each glimpse of the odd makes me giggle with cheer.

So here I will wander, with whimsy in mind,
For every strange find is a joy well-defined.
With each little step, I'm not just alive,
I'm dancing with chaos, it's how I thrive!

The Horizon of Home

The edges of comfort, they wiggle and sway,
Each peek through my window, a brand new array.
What's that on the lawn? A creature so bold,
Exploring the grass, a tale to be told.

It hops like a rabbit, yet sportier still,
With sneakers and shades, it's quite the free will.
A flip and a flop, oh what a delight,
Who knew my backyard was host to such fright?

But laughter erupts as it fumbles the dance,
With every wild twirl, it gives life a chance.
In skies that are changing, horizons expand,
Embracing the wild, I'll take it by hand.

So here I shall sit, in this chaos divine,
With critters and laughter, my stars will align.
For home is more than just walls or a key,
It's chuckles and wonders that set my heart free.

Lurking Within the Frame

A shadow dances, quite absurd,
It waves its arms, a funny bird.
Behind the glass, it makes a face,
Inviting all to join the chase.

The cat is puzzled by the show,
He jumps and twirls, puts on a glow.
What lies beyond that silly glass?
A world of giggles, will it pass?

With shoes all lined up by the door,
I wonder what those socks are for.
Are they a sign? A message true?
Or just a prank from shoe-less too?

The doorknob laughs; it creaks and spins,
Unlocking mischief, where it begins.
With every turn, the laughter grows,
In our own realm where silliness flows.

Treading the Unfamiliar Path

The path ahead is wild and weird,
With dancing leaves and frogs that cheered.
My feet, they trip on roots and stones,
A journey full of funny tones.

The squirrels gossip in the trees,
As I trip over a couple of bees.
They buzz and laugh; I twist and turn,
For every stumble, my heart does yearn.

A sign that says, 'Do Not Go Here,'
I read it twice, but still don't fear.
With every step, I grin and sway,
A giggling fool who's lost his way.

The end of this path is yet unknown,
With promises of ice cream cones.
I'll follow laughter, chase the fun,
And maybe trip on everyone.

The Tension of Choices

Two paths fork at the apple tree,
One smells like pie, the other, brie.
Should I devour, should I explore?
Oh choices dance like never before.

Left or right? The tension mounts,
As ants debate, while others count.
Do I pick fruit or chase a bug?
Life's little joys, they give a hug.

Sticky fingers or muddy shoes?
Either way, I cannot lose.
Shall I dance with the bees in flight?
Or take a nap 'til fades the light?

With decision made, I skip along,
Each option wrapped in silly song.
For in this chaos, joy is found,
With laughter echoing all around.

The Quiet Call of Adventure

A whisper floats from the bushy leaves,
It giggles soft and then it heaves.
'Come play with us,' it seems to say,
Adventure calls in a funny way.

From ladders built of imagination,
To forests filled with strange creation.
I wear a crown made out of toast,
Conquering lands where fairies boast.

With each step on a bouncy trail,
I find a dragon, soft and pale.
He tickles me with wings so wide,
In the realm of dreams, I joyfully slide.

The quiet call, so sweet and bright,
Guiding me into the whimsical night.
Every giggle, every cheer,
In this adventure, there's nothing to fear.

A Glimmer Outside

A shadow with a floppy hat,
Maybe it's a clever cat!
A gust of wind makes curtains sway,
What chaos lurks outside today?

I peek out with a cereal spoon,
Is that a raccoon dancing to a tune?
My neighbor's got a man in a box,
Should I call the cops or offer socks?

Children giggle, running past,
A parade of ducks makes me laugh fast.
A slinky dog rolls down the lane,
Who knew such fun could cause such fame?

I'll venture out, face the surprise,
With rainbow socks and sparkly eyes.
Each step a hint of mystery,
What else will this day reveal to me?

The Great Unfolding

A doorbell rings with glee and surprise,
I answer to find a clown with pies!
He juggles fruit with style and flair,
And asks me for a chair to share.

The garden gnomes are all in rows,
Yet they move like dancers, heaven knows!
They twirl and leap amidst the blooms,
A ballet of laughter fills the rooms.

A book that flits like a buttered bee,
Tells tales of mischief, wild and free.
Each page a portal to silly delight,
Inviting me to join in the flight.

And just when I think it's all but done,
Out pops a rabbit with a water gun!
"Join the spout and splash with cheer!"
Ah, what a day, I'll stick right here!

Portals to Possibility

A crack in the wall reveals a door,
With a sign that's marked, 'Adults No More!'
I peer inside—a realm of cheer,
Where socks are used to make a beer.

The kitchen's filled with candy rain,
Where spoons dance freely, all insane.
Here, broccoli sings sweet lullabies,
In this land with marshmallow skies.

Around a table, friends all meet,
With talking chairs that wiggle and greet.
A pie that fights back when you slice,
"It's just a game, roll the dice!"

Will I ever return to my bed?
Or stay in this land where fun is fed?
Each moment's a whim, nothing is bland,
In this world of joy, I take a stand!

Crossroads of Wonder

At the crosswalk, I spy a turtle,
In sunglasses, he's quite the hurdle.
With a grin, he shouts, 'Walk with me!'
Both of us aim for the nearest tree.

A ladybug on roller skates,
Zooms past with hopes, it doesn't wait!
While a snail challenges the clock,
"Beat me now! I'm the king of the block!"

A traffic light flashes a vibrant blue,
"Dance now, friends! This song's for you!"
So we shake our bodies under the sun,
Who knew waiting could be so much fun?

And as the day draws to a close,
With twinkling lights and a fanfare hose.
I'll laugh and ponder what I have learned,
Life's a party—when it's truly turned!

The Invitation to Wander

A sock on the floor, a cat on the wall,
I step out the door, and hear a loud call.
The neighbor's lawn gnome points straight at my shoe,
With a grin and a wink, he says, "Come on, too!"

Spring breezes are teasing, the squirrels have a race,
They're plotting and scheming, oh what a wild chase!
A mailbox that chuckles as I walk on by,
It says, "Don't be shy, give the mailbox a try!"

A puddle reflects all the silly delight,
I jump with a splash, oh, what a bold sight!
Then a bird darts above, with a wink and a cheer,
It says, "Let's explore! The world's waiting here!"

Adventure is calling, it's time to embrace,
The wonders of laughing, in this quirky place.
With every step forward, the sun's shining bright,
The world's a grand circus, oh what a delight!

Where Dreams Meet Daylight

In sleepy pajamas, I shuffle outside,
Where shadows play tricks and the squirrels collide.
The garden gnomes gossip, they're in on the joke,
As roses blush red under sun's playful poke.

I caught a mad wind that just wouldn't behave,
It ruffled my hair like a restless wave.
A butterfly landed and fluffed at my cheek,
It whispered, "Come dance! Don't be such a freak!"

The neighbor's dog joins, he's leading the charge,
With a bark and a leap, oh, he's living large!
A tulip sarcastically sways in the breeze,
"Where are you going? Come hang with the trees!"

So I twirl and I hop, let my spirit soar free,
In a land full of laughter, where funs the decree.
With sunshine like candy and skies painted blue,
In this joyful adventure, there's always room for two!

Threshold Whispers

The doormat greets with a smirk and a sigh,
"Leave your worries outside, let your giggles fly high!"
A mailbox named Max raises a brow with a grin,
"Knock, knock on the world, let the fun times begin!"

The front hedge leans close, whispering tales of delight,
"Did you see the lost shoe that danced last night?"
Garden fairies chuckle, as daisies align,
"Step lightly and quickly, for laughter is divine!"

A wiggle of bumblebees, buzzing their tune,
Tell tales of sweet nectar beneath the bright moon.
I laugh with the roses, they're blooming with glee,
This gateway of giggles is just waiting for me!

So I skip and I scurry, a smile on my face,
In this realm of whispers, where joys interlace.
Step over the threshold, let silliness roam,
In the curious kingdom, you can always come home!

The Invitation of Dawn

As dawn tiptoes in, with a laugh on its face,
It brings out the crocuses, a colorful race.
The sun sneaks a peek, stretching out with a yawn,
Saying, "Rise up, sleepyheads, let's dance on the lawn!"

The birds start a concert, with tunes that enthrall,
While bugs take their seats like they're at the ball.
A worm in the grass knows the giddy ol' theme,
"Come hop into sunshine, and live out the dream!"

Bouncing and giggling, the daisies all sway,
They whisper sweet secrets of wondrous playdays.
"Catch mists on your toes, let your laughter ring loud,
In this bright, silly morning, let's gather a crowd!"

So I join in the fun, with a skip and a shout,
Finding joy in the petals, with nary a doubt.
With each dewy step in this land of pure cheer,
The invitation of dawn makes the whole world appear!

A Breeze Through Cracked Glass

In the hall, a cat takes flight,
Chasing shadows, what a sight!
The dog just sighs, lays on the mat,
Dreaming of being a bold acrobat.

A breeze sneaks in through gaps and cracks,
Tickling noses, catching snacks.
Mom yells 'Stop that!' with a laugh,
While Dad just grins, enjoying the gaffe.

Socks go missing, where'd they flee?
Dancing elves? Can't let it be!
We set a trap with cheese and flair,
But all we catch is thin air.

The world outside may hold its charm,
But inside's where we raise the alarm.
With giggles loud and laughter wide,
Our cracked glass keeps joy inside.

Passageways of the Heart

In the kitchen, cookies fly,
Flour on cheeks, oh me, oh my!
A recipe lost, but we don't care,
Just make a mess; it's magic in the air.

Baking soda? Who needs that!
Spatulas dance as the dog sits flat.
Mom's on a mission, her hair a storm,
With math that bends all rules of norm.

Sibling rivalries, oh what a show,
Dancing around, chases in tow.
Joy spills over, like milk, oh dear,
And laughter's the only thing we hear.

In our hearts, the secret lies,
In laughter, love, and baking pies.
Our passageways wind and twist,
Full of giggles, a cherished tryst.

Ascent into Mystery

The stairs creak loud as I get brave,
What's lurking there? A ghost or wave?
Is it a monster? Or just a sock?
With daring heart, I take stock.

A broomstick horse? I can't deny,
Galloping boldly, I soar the sky!
Mom's voice calls, "Time to come down!"
But who would stop the knight with a crown?

My sister hides behind the plant,
With giggles loud, oh what a chant!
We plot and scheme till the sun goes low,
Adventurers lost in the world we know.

Every corner holds a surprise,
A shoe, a glove, or ancient fries.
In every nook, a tale we spin,
To rise again, then dive back in.

The Nest of Possibilities

Under the table, a nest we make,
Cushions and snacks, oh what a break!
It's a castle tear-down, a fortress of fun,
With whispers shared till the day is done.

Adventure awaits in each hidden spot,
A world of wonders and things forgot.
We craft secret plans with silly maps,
And giggle at all the playful mishaps.

A pillow fort stands proudly tall,
While dust bunnies dance and hear our call.
The cat looks on with a judgy stare,
But she'll join in when we're unaware.

Our nest holds dreams and laughter bright,
Where every moment feels just right.
With imagination soaring high,
In our little world, we touch the sky.

The Call of the Open Air

The wind whispers secrets, quite absurd,
As my cat pretends it's a fearless bird.
I laugh as she tumbles, a playful sight,
While squirrels conspire in daylight's light.

The mailman arrives with packages galore,
I hide in the bushes, can't take it anymore!
His puzzled expression brings joy to my day,
An uninvited guest, in my own little play.

Faint Sounds from Afar

I hear strange noises drifting through the air,
A lawnmower roaring! Oh, what a scare.
Is it a monster, or just my old neighbor?
Both of them buzzing like some wild labor!

The dog barks loudly, his mind's in a whirl,
As he spots a cat giving an elegant twirl.
Faint sounds of chuckles, a clash, and a spill,
Life's outside drama, it gives me a thrill.

Uncharted Territories

I step outside wearing mismatched socks,
Exploring the vastness—my home is a box!
The garden gnomes whisper, or so I believe,
As weeds plot revenge, like a sneaky reprieve.

Adventure awaits past the tall garden fence,
With neighbors who dance, they don't have a sense.
Dodging the ice cream truck, it's a race,
With sticky fingers, I join in the chase!

The Promise of Tomorrow

Tomorrow's a promise, full of delight,
But today's just chaos, try as I might.
The hose is a serpent, the kids in a splash,
Water fights break out; it's such a mad clash!

Unruly plants wave like they're at a fair,
I trip on a garden rake, oh, what a scare!
Yet laughter erupts like pops from a fizz,
Tomorrow's adventures? Oh, what will it give?

A Portal to Possibility

A creaky step leads to the floor,
Where socks and shoes are lost in lore.
A cat with eyes of dubious might,
Is plotting schemes well into the night.

The doormat's dirty, it shows some charm,
As it welcomes all with open arms.
Who knew the world could call so loud,
When you've just mastered napping proud?

A wiggle of a tail, a sparkle of light,
What's this? A squirrel? Oh what a sight!
The mailbox hums with secrets galore,
While lawn gnomes grin with tales of yore.

Unlocking an adventure, a twist of fate,
For every step is a new debate.
Flip-flops flip and the wind will tease,
Outside awaits, with giggles and sneeze.

Paths of Discovery

A garden path that's twisted and bent,
Where daisies whisper their secret scent.
The hedge is trimmed in cartoonish style,
If only bushes could walk a mile!

The neighbor pets a suspicious snail,
While bicycles weave like a fairy tale.
An adventurous duck takes to the stream,
While kids in puddles chase their dream.

What lies ahead? A tree or a wall?
A distant giggle or a sudden fall?
Each corner turned, a wiggle and dance,
Life's little jest becomes a chance.

With every step, the grass gets taller,
In search of treasures and wild calls of a holler.
A journey grand awaits each foot,
When paths of laughter are your pursuit.

Veils of Anticipation

What lurks behind the drapes so worn?
A sock puppet army, freshly born!
They plot their take-over with marshmallow eyes,
As cereal raids become their surprise.

The fridge hums softly a secret tune,
Inviting the brave with a midnight boon.
A leftover pizza, a slice to behold,
Transforms a warrior, both fierce and bold.

Will it be ice cream or pickle delight?
Such difficult choices in the dead of night.
With snacks in hand, the raid's begun,
Tomorrow's breakfast? Oh well, more fun!

As shadows blend with the sparkling hush,
Vigilant eyes fixate on the rush.
In the living room, shenanigans reflect,
In the quiet chaos of dreams unchecked.

The Call of the Wild

Outside a critter does a dance,
A squirrel with dreams of epic chance.
The dog next door gives a hearty bark,
As he plans to steal an adventure arc.

With wind in my face and shades on tight,
I race with glee, a comical sight.
Tree branches wave like hands in cheer,
Join the parade, all land creatures near!

Oh look! A butterfly, bright and bold,
Flapping about like it's mid-foretold.
I chase it down, through grasses and vines,
Chasing giggles and wild sunshine signs.

The world outside is absurdly grand,
With treasure hunts through shifting sand.
Every leaf rustles a contagious call,
To join the fun, come one, come all!

Open Gates to Wonder

There's a garden gnome with a grin,
Who insists that magic is just within.
He waves at the mailman each day at noon,
Claiming he dances under a cartoon moon.

A squirrel named Larry steals all the snacks,
While a parrot nearby loudly relax.
Every visitor wonders what's out of sight,
But the gnome just chuckles, 'It's all in your flight.'

A trampoline bounces at the edge of the lawn,
With kids airborne like they're gazing upon.
The laughter erupts, it's a sweet serenade,
As neighbors just shake their heads in charade.

There's a hidden swing that creaks with delight,
Where dreams take off and take glorious flight.
So join in the fun where wonders abound,
And keep your feet light – don't touch the ground!

The Space Between Us

A cat on the fence eyes a chicken with glee,
While the dog in the yard dreams of goldfish and tea.
They swap nothings with furrowed brows of utmost concern,
Which leads to a chase, but it's time to adjourn.

The postman arrives with a letter of fate,
But instead finds a shoe that was left by a mate.
He chuckles and thinks, 'This job's quite absurd!'
As he tosses it back saying, 'Guess it's preferred!'

Across the way, garden gnomes start to chat,
Scheming plans for a snack or a spat.
They laugh over coffee, then quietly conspire,
And plot how to sneak past the very wide wire.

So if you stroll past where the chaos does bloom,
You'll know that delight hangs inside of the room.
With every flip and every stride so true,
Just remember the laughter that bridges us two!

Close Encounters of Afternoons

The lawn chairs gather in a semicircle wide,
As neighbors exchange tales of worlds that collide.
One claims to have spotted a UFO fly,
While another swears squirrels can leap through the sky.

A frisbee takes flight, but lands on a roof,
Launching an argument devoid of all proof.
They debate for an hour, then laugh till they're sore,
When the frisbee returns from the neighbor next door.

An ice cream truck jingles its sweet call of fate,
And all come together, the kids and their mates.
With sticky fingers wrapped around melting treats,
They gossip in flavors much sweeter than feats.

And just as the sunlight begins to depart,
The adventures unwind, like a love-worn chart.
So let's not forget the fun afternoons,
Where laughter and stories dance under balloons!

Windows to Unwritten Journeys

Peering through glass, what do we behold?
A parade of mischief, both brave and bold.
A dog with a hat, and a cat with a cape,
Form a duo so grand, it's beyond any shape.

They scheme through the day, then nap in the sun,
In a world made of dreams where everything's fun.
The neighbors all wonder what secrets they share,
As shadows rush by like a whimsical flair.

A bicycle races with wheels made of cheese,
While the mailbox sings lullabies with a seize.
Children in capes launch themselves from the swing,
While the home's very walls giggle at everything.

So if you peer closer, remember this fight:
Life's full of magic when you open your sight.
Unwritten journeys lie just past your glance,
Where laughter and joy make us all take a chance!

www.ingramcontent.com/pod-product-compliance
Lightning Source LLC
Chambersburg PA
CBHW060143230426
43661CB00003B/548